"The undressed is vulgar -
the nude is pure."

Robert G Ingersoll

First published in Great Britain in 1997 by
Chameleon Books
106 Great Russell Street
London WC1B 3LJ

Copyright for text © DC Publications Ltd

CIP data for this title is available from the British Library

ISBN 02339 9182 4

Book and jacket design by Generation Studio

Printed by Graficas Zamudio Printek in Spain.

André Deutsch Ltd is a subsidiary of VCI plc.

ACKNOWLEDGEMENTS:
A special thanks to Steve Muncey, Paul Sudbury,
Mel and Caroline Warde.

Adrian Murrell and the guys at Allsport,
all keen streaker fans across the country and the man
who made it all possible - Tim Forrester

PHOTOGRAPH ACKNOWLEDGEMENTS
ALLSPORT
COVER PICTURE : GARY M. PRIOR

ADRIAN MURRELL. PAGES : 52-57 64 99 102 106/107
RUSSELL CHEYNE. PAGES : 48/49 62 62
VANDYSTADT. PAGES : 10/11 12/13
DAVID CANNON. PAGES : 14/15
CLIVE BRUNSKILL. PAGES : 18 88/89
GARY M.PRIOR. PAGE : 19
PASCAL RONDEAU. PAGE : 25
DAVE ROBERTS. PAGE : 36
GRAHAM CHADWICK. PAGE : 60
SIMON MILES. PAGES : 82/82
STU FOSTER. PAGES : 86/86
MARK THOMPSON. PAGE : 90

POPPERFOTO PAGES : 9 20 21 24 31-33 40/41 43 46/47 58/59 69 72 76 79
REX FEATURES PAGES: 6/7 16 17 22 27 65 67 70 100

Dedicated to
John and Anna Valentine and all the
regulars at the Chequers, Watlington, Oxon.

Like all public performances; streaking has its anti-squads.

But the phenomenon definitely has its fans too - plenty of them and it wouldn't be normal if it were otherwise! But why do people streak? To show off their beautiful sleek bodies (!) ; as a dare; a crack at media attention; a bit of tipsy skylarking and/or merely carried away by the sheer exuberance of the occasion and making a spur-of-the-moment dash for joyous freedom?

Whatever the motivation, I sincerely believe that streaking has been, and I hope will continue to be, a carefree, non-violent, to heck-with-it all show of a little gentle madness, exhibitionism and free-spiritedness.

I know of one perfect example which delighted me. I woke up one Christmas morning full of the usual feelings of special anticipation and discovering snow had fallen. What joy! Without a moments thought or hesitation I cast pyjama's to the wind, skipped into the garden with a cry of delight and frolicked in the invigorating cold snow like a happy puppy. What a perfect way to start the day.

In public or in private, streakers, generally, do not mean to offend. There are much worse things going on in our world which we should be offended by and streaking is not one of them.

I hope you will enjoy this collection of streakers as it should be appreciated. As a bit of harmless entertainment performed by very normal people who go to work dressed smartly and help the older generation to cross the road.

Be good now!!

ERICA ROE

Eurovision Dong Contest 1
1st entry - Nil Points

SOME NOTABLE NUDISTS

THE VERY FIRST STREAK

The first streaker originated in, of all places, Coventry. Lady Godiva, who lived between 1040 and 1085, was the wife of the Earl of Leofric. She rode naked through the streets to obtain from her husband tax relief for the town. Peeping Tom, the one man who failed to stay indoors during her streak, was struck down blind.

"Lady Godiva you don't sweat much for a fat lass, do you?"

ROE'S RUGBY TACKLE

Britain's most famous streaker, Erica Roe, bared her 40 inch chest at Twickenham during a televised rugby match between England and Australia in 1981. Unfortunately, it wasn't her ticket to fame and fortune. However she said: "I have no regrets. I put a lot of smiles on a lot of faces." Eventually, she went on to after-dinner speaking at rugby clubs and settled down to married life in Portugal, and occasionally writing forewords for books on Streakers.

Erica donating her shirt to a captive audience.

'You forgot your coat sir'.

TWICKENHAM TITTERS

In April, 1974 accountant Michael O'Brien, 26, dashed naked across Twickenham during a home international rugby match for a £10 bet. Pictures of the Christ-like figure being caught by PC Bruce Perry, who famously whipped off his helmet to cover O'Brien's helmet became some of the most enduring of that decade. "It was a cold day," said the PC, "and I can tell you, he had nothing to be proud of." Ironically, some 20 years later those same pictures re-emerged as part of British Telecom's Phoneday advertising campaign, being splashed on hoardings as, "It's 1 to remember."

SERIAL STREAKERS

This particular affliction seems to affect the males of the species and two men in particular. Tony Buckmaster makes a habit of letting it all hang out at racecourses. He streaked at Ascot twice, once at Cheltenham, five times at Epsom, including in front of the Queen Mother in 1988, and twice at Sandown. He wants to fulfill a dream - by completing the grand slam and streaking at the big one - the Arc de Triomphe.

More infamous still is Mark Roberts, who shocked his widest audience yet and made temperatures soar on Richard Madeley and Judy Finnigan's This Morning TV show. Weatherman Fred Talbot was in the middle of his broadcast when Mark produced a full frontal outlook as he popped out of the water and onto the floating map of Britain moored in Liverpool's Albert Dock. The broadcast had to be stopped and Mark, a father of two, said: "I bet Fred did not expect to see a full moon at this time of day." Mark developed his habit of streaking at sports events when he was working in Hong Kong and only three months prior to his "guest" appearance on This Morning had been banned from all football grounds in Britain by Liverpool magistrates after stripping off during a Liverpool FA Cup tie at Anfield. He also showed the world his niblick when he streaked at St Andrews immediately after John Daly had captured the Open Golf Championship in 1995, replete with an arrow pained on his back pointing towards his derrier, accompanied by the words "19th hole". He has since been the subject of a documentary and his ambition, he says, is to streak at the US Superbowl.

'Please get that thing out of my arse.

'Excuse me sir, the missus is a big fan of yours. Could you autograph mine for her?'

That was close,
Cliff was just about
to sing again.

TWO SETS TO LOVE

The tennis at Wimbledon might have been a tad boring in 1996, but it was soon livened up by pretty Melissa Johnson who claimed her 15 minutes of fame by streaking across Centre Court before the start of the men's final, bringing a smile to the faces of Richard Krajicek and Mal Washington. Still, streaking runs in the family, so to speak, as it was later revealed that mother Caroline had taken off her top at a Rolling Stones concert and ran naked across the neighbour's herbaceious borders in the 60s and Melissa's rebellious sister Lydia who was involved in a St Trinians style rampage at her school!

"This is a very serious matter madam, you are hereby charged with bringing some interest to the game of tennis. Oh, and a word of advice. Avoid the ladies changing rooms, Martina has just finished her doubles game".

RECORD STRIP

Gaslight Records store in Melbourne soared to the top of the charts in October 1990 when manager Jeff Harrison offered to give away free discs if punters either sang, danced - or stripped off! Most decided it was easiest to peel off their clothes and in no time at all the store was bulging with...well, bulges. To liven things up Jeff also laid on a band - who were also starkers - and soon the whole store was shakin' it all about. "We had one of these nude days before, but it didn't work out anywhere near as well" said Jeff. "Perhaps the hot weather has something to do with it this time."

Andie McDowell auditioning for
'4 Weddings and a Funeral'.
She got the part.

STREAKERS PITCH IN

During a Tottenham Hotspur versus Manchester United game in 1991 televised live on television, a naked couple made a naked dribble to the centre circle whjere they unfurled a huge banner bearing the emblem "World Peace". While the man escaped into the crowd, club stewards hurried on to the pitch and caught the girl, covering her up quickly. Unfortunately, the covers slipped off just as the TV director decided to zoom in on the incident!

FROM THE HART

It was a case of Gulf War Syndrome when shapely Jocelyn Graham, 24 and her pal Robin Denton dashed naked onto the pitch at the Tottenham-Manchester United New Year clash at White Hart Lane in 1991. "I decided to do it as a way of drawing attention to the crazy war that could soon break out," said Jocelyn, who added that she and Robin were planning to take their peace crusade to Saddam Hussein in Iraq. "But I promise I won't streak in front of him," she added, "I hear he's excited enough already!"

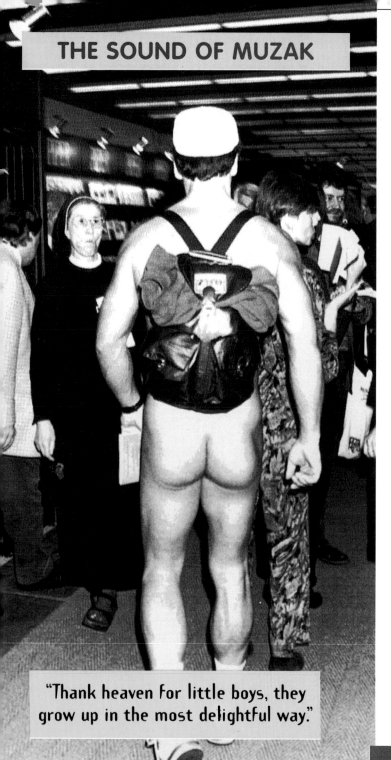

"Thank heaven for little boys, they grow up in the most delightful way."

A BOOB AND A HALF

Police had their hands full trying to arrest a young girl who flashed her 40-inch boobs at a Bristol City soccer match in 1987. The officers gave chase but the girl dodged into the crowd and when the officers finally nabbed their woman, it turned out to be the wrong one! The boob was understandable as the victim, 20-year-old Mona Dubland, bore a striking resemblance to the flasher, Maria Palfrey, who, it turned out, was Mona's best friend. "I wanted to do a full streak," said Maria, " but decided against it as I did not want to miss my 21st birthday party arranged for after the match."

Mona was dragged down to the local Police station and freed after they checked her out. "There was no shortage of volunteers," said a Police spokesman.

A football team with but one collective thought - though even one is debatable

LOOKING FOR A STRIP

Football teams all need a strip to play in, but a team in Rome threatened to adopt disticly pink team colours. Trained by former Roma defender Enzo Romano, the men of the Italian National Striptease Football Federation have become the butt, so to speak, of many a joke in their homeland. "We want to be taken seriously," said striker, Nicola "Rhinestone Cowboy" Devito. "We'll be playing for charity and we're all fit men." Unfortunately, that won't be happening, at least until they have sorted out their team colours and a sponsor to supply their kit.

THERE'S MY WIFE!

Dave Sherwood and his mates, playing for Sorrel FC in a Sunday league clash near Ipswich in April 1983, couldn't believe their eyes when an attractive brunette "did an Erika" across the pitch in front of 300 spectators. Dave got an even greater shock when he realised that the streaker was his wife, Jan, who was going topless for a bet with her friends. Dave said: "I couldn't believe she actually did it. I wouldn't have minded but we lost 3-0 into the bargain!"

NEW YORK'S FINEST?

Two New York police officers were thrown off the force after a naked rampage in a hotel during a convention to honour murdered colleagues. Wayne Hagmaier and James Morrow, the latter nicknamed "Naked Man" because of his willingness to remove his clothes at parties, slid down a beer-soaked escalator hand rail with no clothes on in front of cheering comrades at New York's Hyatt Regency Hotel in May 1996. Senior police officials said they were the worst offenders during a night of mayhem during which New York's so-called finest battled in hotel corridors with fire extinguishers and forced an evacuation of guests by triggering fire alarms. One policewoman also took part in a wet T-shirt competition and was then stripped of her badge when she tested positive for cocaine in a subsequent drug test.

"It's ok officer, I'm only protesting about my small holding".

FOR THE SAKE OF ART

Only New York-based photographic artist Spencer Tunick could convince 50 people to conduct a mass streak in the freezing cold air of an early winter morning. In February 1995 he asked 23 volunteers to help him launch a London exhibition by stripping off in Mayfair in London's West End. First they lay down in the street in groups of five in the shape of stars for a piece called "The Intellect and Valour of Britain" before streaking across Berkeley Square where they lay down with their ears to the tarmac for another chilly photo shoot. "I think it's great to be part of a work of art," said one volunteer through chattering teeth. Tunick repeated the stunt on a freezing cold November morning in New York with 50 volunteers who had responded to a newspaper advert. He had them all lying naked in a gutter for 60 seconds until their goosebumps became their most prominent features!

BIT PART

The five thespians concerned treated their part in Peter Greenaway's exhibition as just another day's work, but any shivers they had were not from nerves, they were caused by the chilly draughts in the Hayward Gallery. The controversial film director, painter and writer required the actors to sit naked in glass boxes, closed in on only three sides so members of the public could chat to them. The five nudes were part of a work featuring different themes, changing every day, which was staged in March 1996. On another day there were five actors with red hair, on another five women who had played Juliet, among many others. The display was, according to Greenaway, a comment on how actors are categorised. One actor, Ben Cole, said: "Everybody except the actors seems to be embarrassed. My only concern is that I might catch a cold."

PEKING AT NUDES

In China, nude models were banned from art schools between the 1949 revolution and 1984. Universities and colleges were granted permission to use them again on the grounds that "Nude modelling is pure and beautiful," according to a government spokesman.

FROM RUSSIA WITH LOVE

Smouldering Russian model Ludmila Smits got the schoolboys at Eton all hot and bothered in 1986 when she was hired to help out with Russian language classes - and to pose nude for art students! "The boys at Eton are real gentlemen and anything I can do to help East-West relations pleases me greatly," said Ludmila, who was nicknamed the "Secret Soviet Weapon" by the admiring young Etonians, "I am a democrat and will take off my clothes for anyone!"

THE NAKED TRUTH

The anonymous "Naked Man" doesn't just like to streak, he has to if he wants to make a living. His job is to walk around the streets in his birthday suit. Photographer Philip Moro used the Edinburgh-based Scot for a collection of images for Christmas cards and calenders. In the cards, he can be seen exposing himself in a number of famous locations across Europe, including Salisbury Cathedral, Edinburgh, Berlin, Paris and Amsterdam. For Mr Moro's British collection he got Naked Man to stride starkers down Oxford Street and through Covent Garden, but his artistic antics aren't always allowed to go unchecked. Naked Man was arrested by French Police while posing on the Eiffel Tower, liberal Amsterdam couldn't tolerate him and he spent five hours in a Dutch jail, while in 1989 he was arrested and fined £60 after being collared by the doorman at the Savoy Hotel in London. Naked Man claims that due to a rare medical condition of the skin he cannot wear clothes at any time, although he wore underpants until he was 17 when a Harley Street specialist warned him: "Give them up, or die!"

SMALL LEAD

The crowd was less than impressed with Norman McDonald, lead singer with Kinkystick, when he jumped on a the stage naked in a pub in York in January 1996. They didn't criticise his voice, though, it was something else that had caught their eye - just about. Drinkers pricked Norman's ego by chanting "Peewee" and "Get 'em on" and before long they were pelting the band with ashtrays and beer. The trouble only subsided when pub bosses forced the rioters out into the street and shut the boozer down. Norman, a law student at Dundee, said: "I went on naked because I thought I'd feel less inhibited and we'd perform better."

Silly boy.

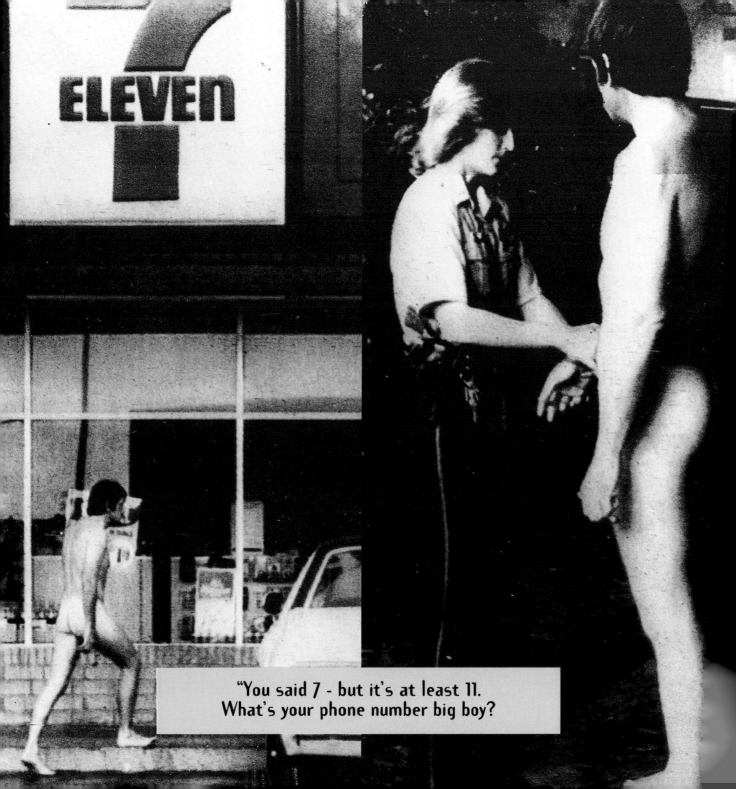

"You said 7 - but it's at least 11.
What's your phone number big boy?

LIFE'S UPS

AND DOWNS

NEW MOONS

Liverpool University's three rugby union teams were disbanded for the rest of the season and a tour to Canada scrapped in March 1990 after a dozen rugby players dropped their trousers and mooned at a posh party. Staring them in the face (even if it was through their legs!) were the University's Vice-Chancellor and a number of his VIP reception guests.

DIRTY DOZEN

Six burly rugby players from Buckinghamshire College in High Wycombe showed their tackles to the world after being stripped naked and left on a busy town centre roundabout after their team had lost. Stunned women motorists watched as the dirty dozen jogged down a steep hill in High Wycombe without even a sock between them. "The men were apparently blamed for losing the match," said a bemused Thames Valley police spokesman.

Arse

'Jabba the Hut's Brother in streak sensation'.

TEAM STREAK

Crewe and Alsager College's rugby team was also banned for the rest of the season and its funds frozen after members of the team and its hockey side pranced naked through the town, in and out of bars and then rampaged through a Chinese restaurant. Damage to property and cars ran into thousands of pounds and many restaurant customers cancelled their order for pork balls!

WHAT A TACKLE

Kim Ward, a rugby player with Bristol-based team Aretians, delighted a bunch of giggling French schoolgirls with a display of his talents on a cross-channel ferry. And they loved his tackle as well as his body swerves - because Kim was dressed only in a pair of flimsy boxer shorts. The girls' teachers were not so impressed, though, and they reported his display to the crew. Kim ended up being convicted for breach of the peace while his team was also banned from travelling on P&O.

BUM SCRUM

The Bude Rugby team found a new and effective way of raising money for their club in 1995 - posing naked for a cheeky calender to raise money for their team. The players raised £1,500 by baring all and every copy was sold out within two weeks. Little did they know that the women's team would follow their example and pose for their own calender in a stunt sponsored by the Daily Mirror. "Now perhaps the men's team will take us more seriously and give us a bigger say in the running of the club," said one calender girl.

TIED UP

Rush-hour traffic in York's city centre was brought to a standstill in 1985 when thirty members of St John Rugby Union Club - all student teachers - decided to teach the general public a lesson in anatomy. They wore their club ties - and nothing else - as they jogged in two columns with their clothes slung over their shoulders. The thin pink lines were soon broken up by the thin blue line when a van load of policemen pounced, but while four offenders were arrested, most managed to streak to freedom.

Four Scottish rugby fans were arrested for exposing themselves. The case was eventually thrown out of court due to lack of material evidence.

"Err mummy, look at that funny man wearing clothes".

RUDE MEMBERS!

Women members of an exclusive golf club were put off their stroke by the antics of naked men lounging on a nearby beach.

Angry club officials at Prince's Club in Sandwich ordered the defiant sun worshippers to cover up or clear off, and they hired security guards, some with vicious dogs, to spell out the message in clear terms.

Two hundred naturists, most of them men, used the secluded beach in front of the Prince's clubhouse in Kent. "The sand dunes bordering the beach are club property and people using them are trespassing," said the club's managing director, "an influx of freaks and exhibitionists are spoiling it for the rest of us."

Security guards handed over leaflets asking the sunbathers to cover up and spare the club ladies' blushes, but dozens of nudes ignored the ban and their leader, retired army Captain Dennis Williams of Broadstairs accused the club of using Gestapo-like tactics. "We've been using the beach for 30 years", he said "and while we do not deny the dunes belong to the club we are disputing the right to deny us access to the beach itself".

ALL FOR A JOB

A streaker who embarrassed Sandy Lyle when he won The Open Championship at Sandwich in 1985, claimed he did it in a desperate bid to get a job! Michael Stock, an army colonel's son, cavorted across the 18th green as Lyle finished his victorious round, and was chased by police before being thrown to the ground by the American golfer, Peter Jacobsen. He had been working for the week at Sandwich but had not had a proper job for four years. "I'm just trying to find a job that allows me to express myself," he said.

LONG LIFE

Supermodels like Naomi Campbell and Linda Evangelista may have a limited shelf life but Yvonne Vinall was Britain's top nude model for 25 years until rheumatoid arthritis forced her to hang up her love handles in October 1996 at the age of 65. During that time she was called upon to stand on tip toes while hanging from the ceiling for one artist, whose work took a year to complete - she developed very strong calves during that particular job; she posed nude for Damien Hirst, whose sculpture of her, entitled "Dismembered in Tunbridge Wells", was sliced in half and pickled in formaldehyde and she was a frequent model at public schools like Eton, Harrow and Westminster. She has about 70 pictures of herself hanging on the walls of her home and she once modelled for a painting that is hanging in Clarence House, home of the Queen Mother. Yvonne would also sometimes do more than just pose - "there are some artists who like sex before they work," she admitted. "I've had affairs with some of my artists, but not all of them!" Oh, and Yvonne would get out of bed for far less than the £10,000 reportedly commanded by Naomi and Linda, but at £12 an hour for the privilege of painting her it still wasn't bad work if she could get it.

"Excuse me miss can I have a look at the CD you're` holding."

TOPLESS TRANCE

Hypnotist Tony Kaye caused controversy when he used his powers to help two shy girls take their tops off!

The blushing babes, Cathy Baker and Alison Green, were nervous about stripping off for the British Miss Topless contest at Skegness in 1982, but after Tony had been to work on them, they happily grinned and bared all. Tony, who was booked to do the main cabaret spot after the contest was told that the two girls had got cold feet (among other things) so he put them in a light hypnotic trance. "They left the room smiling and were full of confidence for the competition," he said. But Tony's antics left the Federation of Ethical Stage Hypnotists fuming: "Our rules forbid anything that brings hypnosis into disrepute," said chairman Peter Casson. They couldn't complain about the quality of Tony's work, though. Cathy Baker came in 1st!

EMERGENCY CALL

On December 9 1986, pretty newscaster Wendy Buckingham, a reporter with Radio Devonair in Exeter, kept a dark secret from her listeners - she wasn't wearing any knickers.

The 30-year old read the morning bulletin in her nightie and furry slippers after receiving an emergency call from her bosses at the station. "I pulled on a coat over my nightie and it wasn't until I got in to work that I realised I had left my knickers off," she said. "I was ever so embarrassed, but there were only four minutes to the 7am news so I didn't have time to do anything about it."

DON'T PRICK YOURSELF!

Professional gardener John Grosvenor has to be careful when he's around rose bushes, because he likes to work in the nude.

The green-fingered naturist skips about starkers round the gardens of posh suburbs although he always seeks permission from his employers first. If granted, John gets to tackle his chores with his tackle out!

"It's a damn sight better that wearing sweaty overalls, although I admit I have to be careful of garden shears or anything else that's sharp," he said. "It makes economic sense too - if I spill paint on myself I can wash it off in the shower without having to worry about cleaning bills. The only hazards are crowds of Peeping Toms around the front gardens," he added. John's clients continue to allow him to strip off though. "Mind you," he says, "most of them are elderly ladies!"

IN THE NUDE GROOVE

Nutty DJ Boothby Graffoe certainly turned the airwaves blue when he stripped off during a live broadcast for Radio Lincolnshire at a health club. Women dressed in leotards started chanting "get em off" and Boothby couldn't resist taking them up on the offer. Listeners jammed the station's switchboard when he announced: "My willy keeps hitting the mike!" Then he created another storm when he declared: "My milk and two sugars are flapping in the wind," as he joined the aerobics session. Boothby was unrepentant though: "The show is meant to be outrageous," he said.

TOPLESS TELLERS

Asset stripping took on a whole new meaning in the financial world when the world's first topless bank opened in Fort Lauderdale, Florida in 1988 in a bid to attract more business. And it worked as customers "chequed out" the four topless tellers - who also sold Coca Cola and souvenirs - in droves. "The only problem is the strong air conditioning," said one teller, Randi Ellis. "I guess you could call it an overdraft!"

JUST THE TICKET

Bus inspector Mike Barber proved just the ticket for a full frontal pose in the "One For The Ladies" section in the pornographic magazine, Fiesta. Copies of the magazine sold out around his home in South Shields, Tyne and Wear as word of the bare-it-all busman spread around the area. Unfortunately, it didn't impress his bosses who gave Mike a rough ride over his saucy pictures. "I'm not ashamed of them but with all the fuss I'm worried about my job," said Mike. "It's only because I am an inspector who has to deal with the public that such an issue is being made of it."

CUTTING A NAKED DASH

Royal gardener Terry Creedon dished out an unexpected surprise when he streaked across Windsor Castle lawns in 1987 in protest after his boss ticked him off for wearing ripped jeans. Creedon was sacked for startling coachloads of foreign tourists who happened to be touring the grounds!

BLUSH HOUR

In 1988 a busty blonde perked up tired commuters on London's Victoria Line tube when it was stopped between stations by a mechanical problem. As temperatures soared in the summer heat, the bronzed teenage beauty calmly stripped off to the waist and, smiling, pushed her way to the front of the train. "We were already hot and bothered," said one passenger. "Then this extremely attractive lady suddenly revealed all. What a tonic. But so many people followed her to the front carriage it took 10 minutes for the train to unload when it finally reached Green Park station." London Transport said: "She kept passengers happy while we sorted out our operational problem. We could certainly do with her again!"

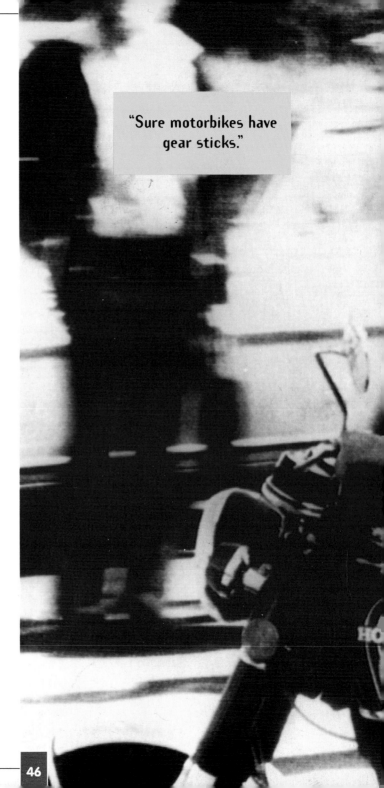

"Sure motorbikes have gear sticks."

"Sure this is a great ride, but where's your helmet"

The Scottish ugly arse competition.
A bloke's face won it.

HOLIDAY BLUES

STREET SCENE

Office workers in Barcelona were given an amusing treat in the summer of 1984. Dutch tourist Peter Levy was stripped off for a wash and a shave in the rear of his moving caravan when his wife, driving the car, suddenly pulled away from the lights in a busy Barcelona street. Peter was catapaulted backwards and out of the doors into the road, landing at the feet of a group of girls on their way to work. As his unsuspecting wife drove on, a group of Spaniards cheered, clapped and shouted "Ole," while one handed him a cabbage leaf to cover his embarrassment.

THE MOONIES

They take their bodies seriously on the sun-worshipping Greek Island of Thasos. When Four young Britons from Coventry "mooned" during a drinking spree on the Island in 1985, they caused fights to break out with the locals and they were promptly arrested and jailed for two years!

BARE BEAST

The Beast of Exmoor returned to scare holidaymakers in the summer of 1987 - only this time it was a man with no clothes on!

Two police forces with tracker dogs ended up searching for the daring stripper who roamed the lonely hills looking for unsuspecting victims. He was never caught, but one local said: "If we ever catch him we'll boot his bare backside out of the area." Ouch!

TRAIN STRIKE

Inter-City commuters travelling through Reading, Berks were treated to a rash of flashes back in 1988. In one astonishing incident, a group of teenagers lifted their skirts in front of a dozing male traveller and rubbed their bare breasts in his face. Then, days later, two saucy teenagers, Rosemary Perrot and Louise Mills, got passengers hot under the collar by revealing their boobs at Reading station.

"We all drank quite a bit because we were celebrating Louise's birthday," said Rosemary. "At the station I lifted my shirt so some young blokes could have a look. The Police thought we were trying to pick up perverts or something - but it wasn't like that."

TRANSPARENT TRUNKS

It would be perfectly understandable if Ralph Appleby now tests all his new bathing trunks in the bath before he hits the beach. The Rolls Royce engineer from Derby was charged with bathing naked on a packed beach on the Costa del Sol in 1982 after fellow holidaymakers had lodged complaints, despite wearing a new pair of cossies.

He spent a night in a cell before being released and returned home. But four years later, when he came back to Spain for another holiday, he was detained for jumping bail and rearrested. He spent 18 days in a Malaga prison before being released on £2,500 bail. Then he returned to Spain to face trial but no verdict was given. After returning home he was eventually told the charges of public indecency had been thrown out. "My trunks did turn transparent, but it was the first time I had worn them so it wasn't really my fault," said the hapless Appleby, who reckoned he was £5,000 out of pocket over the incident.

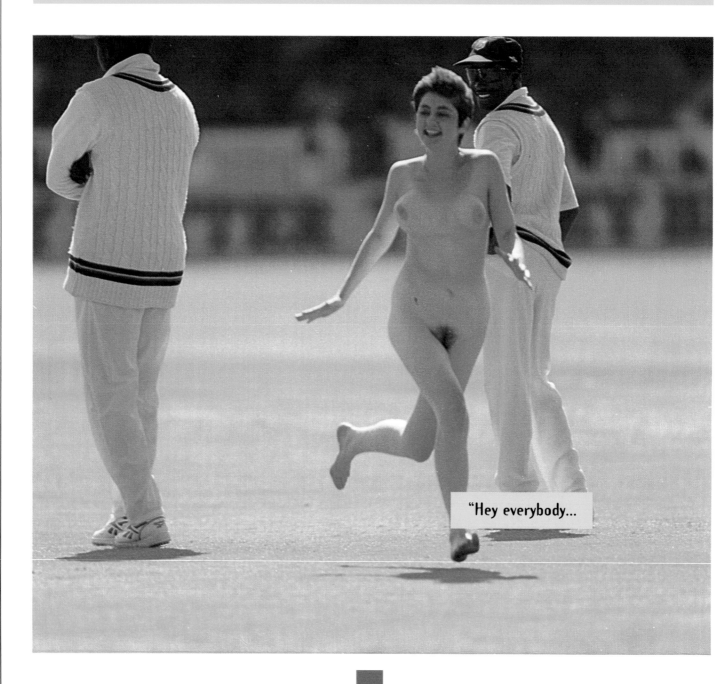

"Hey everybody...

watch this...

"Thank you, thank you, you're so kind".

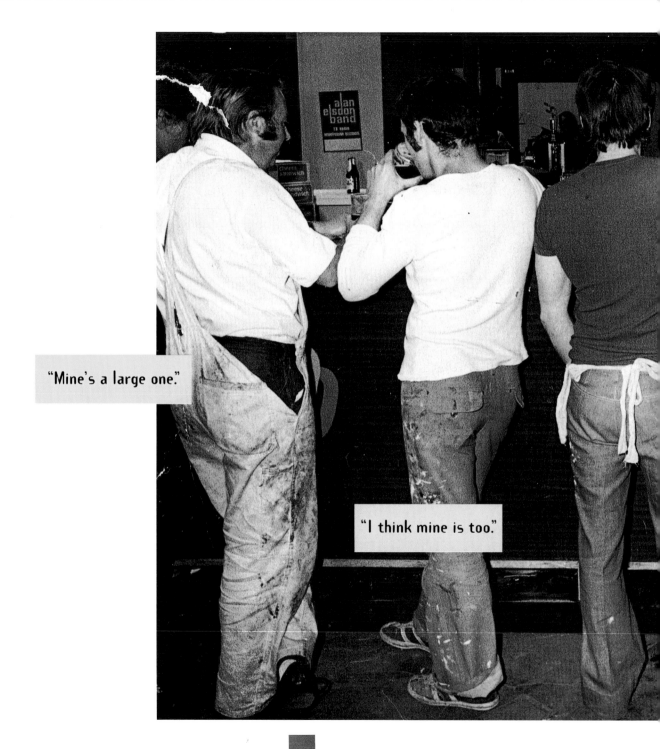

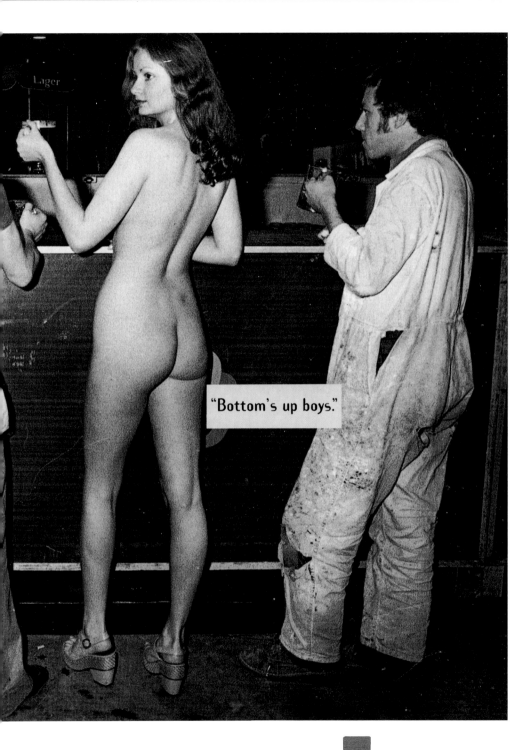

"Bottom's up boys."

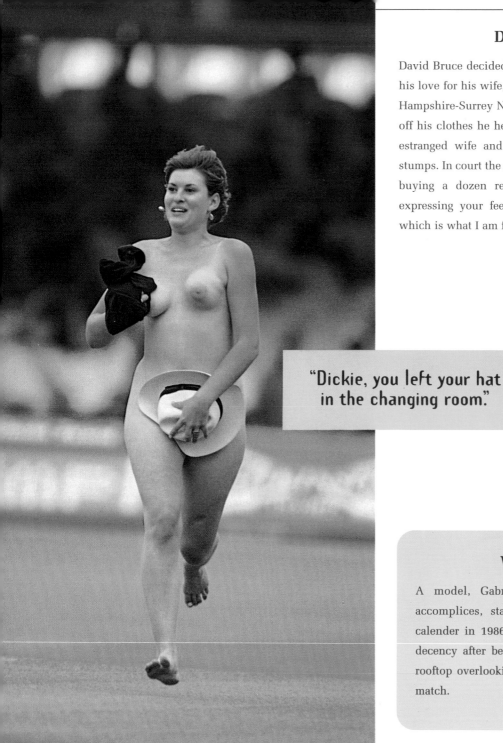

DECLARED OUT

David Bruce decided to try and save his marriage by declaring his love for his wife, Sara, in front of 30,000 cricket fans at the Hampshire-Surrey NatWest cricket final in 1991. After peeling off his clothes he held up a placard declaring his love for his estranged wife and ran across the pitch even vaulting the stumps. In court the magistrate asked him: "Have you ever tried buying a dozen red roses? A more conventional way of expressing your feelings would have cost you about £50 – which is what I am fining you!"

"Dickie, you left your hat in the changing room."

WHAT SPIRIT!

A model, Gabriella Brown, 21, and three male accomplices, staging a publicity stunt for a Vodka calender in 1986, were charged with outraging public decency after being caught doing a topless strip on a rooftop overlooking Lord's cricket ground during a test match.

Essex man with a small job on, makes his way to work.

NOW YOU DON'T

NOW YOU SEE THEM

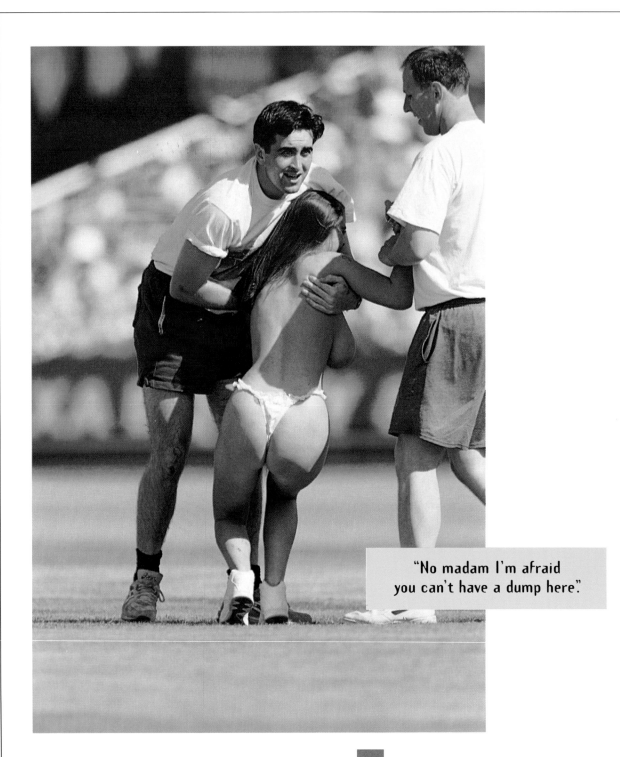

"No madam I'm afraid
you can't have a dump here."

Kathy was supportive during Ian's career.

DRIVING 'EM MAD

SPEEDWAY STREAK

Fans watched in amazement as ex-world speedway champion Michael Lee, Dennis Sigalos and John Cook bared all during a 60 mph streak as a lap of honour at Foxall Stadium in Ipswich 1981. The three riders wore just helmets, boots and safety jackets, but won £10 for their cheek from an American Airforce officer who dared them to do it. "Everyone enjoyed it," said Michael, "but I was a bit worried because it might have been very painful if we had fallen off." The Speedway Control Board was not amused by the naughty stunt though. "I don't think this sort of behaviour should be expected of top sportsmen. It doesn't do speedway any good," said Board manager Dick Brasher.

It might have brought bigger crowds in, though, Dick.

PASSION WAGON

Colin Warriner could not believe his eyes when he saw a van load of naked women speeding down the fast lane of the M5, near Bristol in 1987. The buxom mud wrestling girls struck lewd and suggestive poses for the 21 year-old mechanic and his two mates who swerved and veered onto the hard shoulder in order to get a better view. One of the girls - still topless - then reached across between the two vehicles to hand him a slip of paper with her address and an excited Colin got one of his buddies to take the wheel of his Ford Transit pick-up while he stretched across to try and get in the girls' van. The fun ended when an off-duty policemen used his car-phone to alert a local patrol. After admitting reckless driving, Colin said: "There were two nude women in the front and two in the back - they had everything off and they were flashing the lot. They said they wanted a quick one, so I swapped drivers and at one stage was climbing between the two vehicles. Sadly, I couldn't make it."

TRAFFIC OFFENCE

It was a sweltering hot day and 20-year-old George Stainthorpe decided to strip off his clothes and enjoy a skinny dip in the river. And, oh, how he was enjoying it - until the car in which he had left his clothes was driven off by a friend! George, still naked and joined by another nude swimmer, Davis Spencer, jumped on his motorbike and gave chase. As they sped along roads at speed of up to 60 mph, it wasn't long before they attracted the attention of the local police - especially as they were not only bare, but bare-headed. After being caught and tried at court in Durham, Stainthorpe was fined £50 for careless driving and £10 for...ahem...having no helmet!

"I have this recurring nightmare.
I'm running naked down the street,
and can you believe this...
I'M WEARING GREY SOCKS".

CROWD PLEASERS

COMMUTER SURPRISE

The Brighton Corporation used a revealing way of promoting their arts festival in the summer of 1982 - they got 20-year-old model Tracey Jaine to stand topless, with just a bikini bottom on, just a few feet from the railway line to London and wave a promotional banner at commuters on their way to work.

WINDOW UNDRESSING

Student Joh Morris unwrapped herself in a shop window as a Christmas treat for shoppers in November 1995. Traffic was brought to a halt as people stopped to gawp at Joh's window in a Liverpool furniture store. However, her experiment for a university project came to an end when police came to investigate the disruption and she fled for cover. "I wanted to see people's responses," said Joh, a student at John Moores University. The store manager said: "I thought she was mad but she seemed to have legitimate reasons for doing it so I agreed."

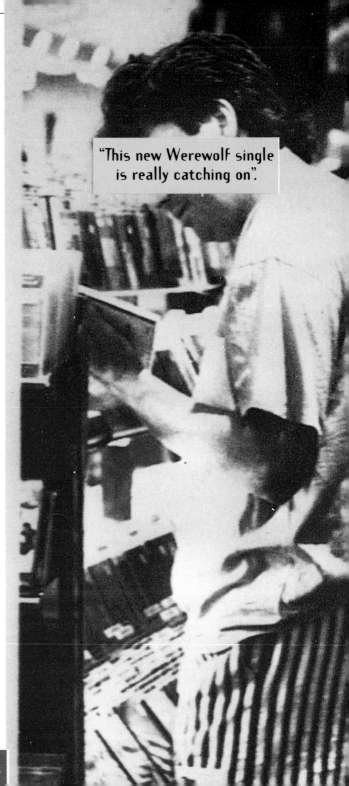

"This new Werewolf single is really catching on".

Tough new rules were called for today in Parliament, as many felt the S&M scene was getting out of hand.

IN A LATHER

A sexy strip by two stunning models at a building exhibition at the NEC in Birmingham in 1985 had to be stopped because it proved <u>too</u> popular. The girls went through a steamy routine that attracted so many punters all the other firms felt like packing up and going home. The two models, dressed in see-through wet T-shirts and revealing swimming costumes, stepped from shower to shower gradually stripping off their clothes in the process. Hundreds of visitors blocked the aisles and trampled over nearby stands to get a better view. Other firms howled in protest and order was only restored when the shower company agreed to halve the number of "strip shows" per day.

NAUGHTY NAUTICAL SEND-OFF

Soldier's wife Dawn Leyman gave the 3,000 troops setting sail for the Falklands in 1982 a flashing send-off when she whipped off her top and tossed her frilly bra to her husband Peter to take to the war. Hundreds of troops packed the ship's rails to cheer her on as they left the dockside. Dawn's mother, Pat, was anything but ashamed of her daughter's "performance": "I wasn't shocked - we're a broadminded family and her little show cheered up the troops and gave them a grand send-off. I'm proud of her," she said.

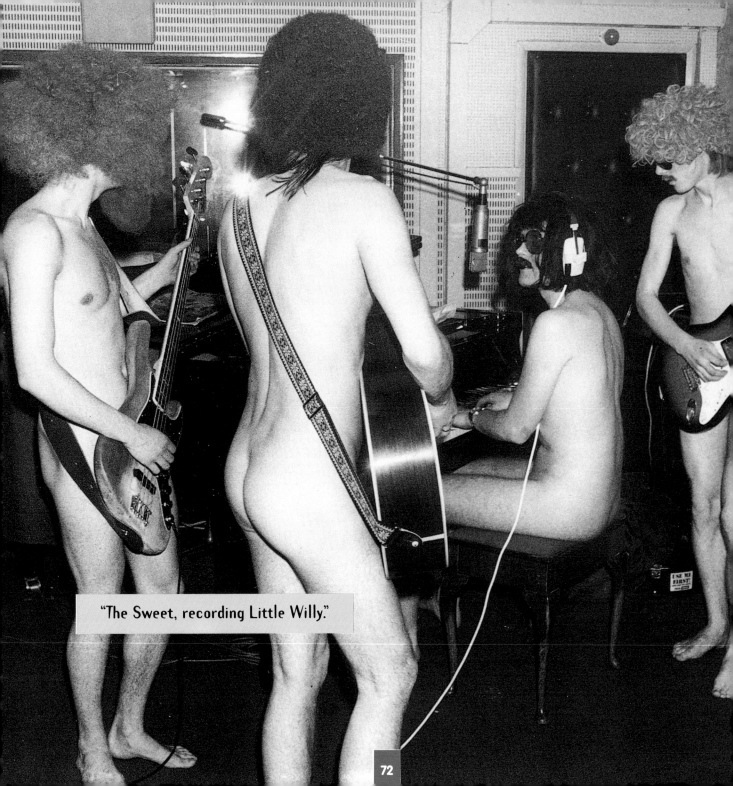

"The Sweet, recording Little Willy."

SKIN ROCK

Dubbed "Rock as God Intended", Nudestock is the world's only naked rock festival and it takes place every year at Turtle Lake, Michigan, one of America's top nudist resorts. Body contact is limited to simple expressions of affection and friendship - even rubbing suntan lotion on your partner in public is prohibited! The festival is a hit every year, attracting crowds of up to 20,000, as is Turtle Lake itself, one of a number of increasing popular nudist resorts. In fact, nude tourism is now the fastest growing sector in the American travel market according to a report in Forbes magazine in 1996.

BUFFS IN THE BUFF

A play at Taunton's Brewhouse Theatre featuring a steamy nude scene in a ladies Turkish bath was watched by an audience of 350 in January 1986, a fact that's not strange in itself except that they were all nude, too! The theatre-goers, who were watching a production of Neil Duncan's comedy, Steaming, did not feel ill at ease though - they were all naturists.

RUDE CELEBRATION

In April 1985 John Hawksworth was, along with millions of others, enjoying live TV pictures from the annual Boat Race, but he was in for a rude shock. He suddenly sat up with a start when he realised that his beloved daughter, Julie, a kissogram girl, was cavorting topless with the winning Oxford crew!

IMITATION STRIP

When a beautiful girl stripped off in a launderette in Bournemouth in 1988, imitating the famous Levi jeans television advert, some customers got into a right lather. She took off all her clothes and put them in a washing machine and sat in her undies while she waited. The police were called but they said she had committed no offence.

OH GODIVA!

Stunning Janie Hamilton proved a big hit when she appeared as Lady Godiva at the village fete in Stokeinteignhead, Devon. Not only was she bareback, she was bare chested too. The buxom blonde created chaos as the male population, including even the local vicar, jammed into the narrow streets in their desperation to catch a glimpse of the 23-year-old model.

BLONDE AMBITION

Gail Ward always wanted to be a Page Three girl and decided to take a shortcut to fame by streaking in a NatWest trophy cricket match between Derbyshire and Nottinghamshire in 1987. In front of 7,000 spectators the 27-year-old blonde whipped off her top and sprinted towards the stumps. "That day I was working on promotions at the ground. I had a glass of wine and just did it," she said. After her big day she continued with promotions and had small parts in the TV series Boon and Chancer as well as becoming MIss 11th Squadron of the Royal Corps of Transport...oh and she made it to The Sun's Page Three, too.

TROUBLE AT WORK

MORTIFIED

It was a case of no more stiffs for assistant undertaker Malcom Dempster when he had to give up work after a nude picture of him appeared in a soft-porn magazine. The picture was taken of him on his honeymoon and sent in by his wife. "I love Malcom so much I wanted everyone to see him like I do," she said. Malcom, though was so ashamed that he quit his job at the funeral parlour. In fact, when he found his wife had sent in the picture he flipped his lid and left home for three days.

THE BRIDE WORE PINK!

The bride and groom downed their underwear Down Under as Ken and Ike Harrison were joined by other suitably undressed guests at their wedding at a nudist beach in Sydney, Australia. The happy couple kept up some traditions, though - by dancing cheek-to-cheek at the reception!

CIVIC STREAK

During an official civic ceremony in Hailsham, Sussex in 1986, Town Crier Dave Rannie announced: "I'd like you to meet a very special man." But as Mayor Ron Harmer appeared, a streaker bounded on to the stage. He shook Mayor Harmer's hand. "How do you do Mr Mayor," said the mystery man solemnly as more than 200 spectators looked on in astonishment. "Very well...how are you," stammered the amazed VIP. Then everyone gasped again as the streaker got down on his hands and knees and kissed the Mayor's feet. The madman was bundled away by police and later released without charge.

"Don't worry it's a sniffer dog trained to check out large packages."

TODAY'S SPECIAL IS...

STREAK - TA TA

A bold as brass car tycoon was thrown out of Michael Caine's old restaurant, Langan's Brasserie, into the freezing cold after he did a strip-tease for a £3,000 bet. Stuart Lancaster streaked among the steaks and the other diners - including soccer boss Malcom Allison - roared with laughter as the burly six-footer dodged the waiters. "We have been trying to raise money for a paralysed boy called Stephen Evans who is in urgent need of treatment," said Stuart. "The lads said they would donate £3,000 towards the appeal if I stripped in Langan's - so I did!"

McDONALD'S BIG DEAL

Customers at the McDonald's in Kentish Town Road in 1987 were amazed when an attractive young girl ordered a burger and then calmly peeled off her skimpy blue top to reveal her very own Big Macs. After finishing her burger she put her clothes back on and walked out. A police spokeman said later: "She has not broken the law but there are a couple of points we'd like to clear up."

SILLY BURGER

Pete Yale proved to be a right silly burger when he strolled into a Wimpy naked and ordered a Kingsize. The stunt, which was the result of a bet with his mates, got the Wimpy staff sizzling, though, as his tattooed backside put ordinary punters off their food. Pete claimed it was all done in a good cause, however, as the proceeds from his bet went to a children's charity.

DYING FOR A LOOK

A Peeping Tom became so excited as he was spying on a nudist colony in Orpington, Kent, he died with his binoculars still clutched in his hand.

The body of the 56-year-old was found in trees bordering the camp after he had suffered a massive heart attack. "I expect his alibi would have been bird watching, but I think I know what sort of birds he was on the look out for," said a spokesman from the colony. "Ironically, if he had waited he could have come in quite legally - we've got our annual open day on Saturday when we allow guests to come in free and have a look around."

WOMEN ONLY

Back before the Iron Curtain came down, a women-only nudist beach on the Baltic coastal resort of Palanga in Lithuania became the centre of the local black market economy - and all because the local force wouldn't go undercover! The local women, trading rare and sought after goods like amber, food, medicine and clothing at highly inflated prices, were allowed to operate unhindered because the local police force was made up mostly of men, and the few women officers there were thought stripping off for their jobs was beyond the call of duty.

"I don't know what you're wearing love, but I think it needs an iron."

STUMPED

CAUGHT BEHIND

A steaker who dashed across the pitch during a ladies match at Adlington Cricket Club near Chorley, Lancs, was "caught behind" when wicketkeeper Evelyn Harding smacked him across his backside with a stump. Village joker Dean Halliwell leapt in the air with pain and retired hurt to the pavillion!

HEAD OVER HEELS

Sheila Nicholls had cricket fans in a spin when she cartwheeled naked across the wicket in front of Ian Botham and 25,000 cricket fans at Lords in an England versus Australia one-day international cricket match in 1989.

LOIN RANGER

Residents in a Wolverhampton suburb were "treated" to the unusual sight of a cowboy flashing his "pistol" one morning. Naturist Derek Gill decided to take an early morning walk dressed in a black Lone Ranger-style mask, overcoat...and nothing else! Words on his mask cheekily referred to his "naked Tonto" which had a piece of blue cord tied to it - just in case anyone didn't notice. He was spotted by a housewife as he took his stroll and soon arrested by posse of Midlands policemen. The court heard that 55 year-old Gill had already been banned from several naturist clubs because of his "unusual" dress sense.

LOVE THY NEIGHBOUR

FIT TO BURST

Residents in Ditton Fields, Cambridge, got used to the sight of seeing keep-fit fanatic Pat Hutt bouncing along the road on her daily jog - trouble was, she insisted on doing all her exercise routines in the nude. Neighbours started a petition to get her evicted from her council home when Pat, who has a 46 inch bust, extended her repertoire to handstands and touching her toes in the buff too. One neighbour said: You can't invite friends round because any minute you expect her to start doing topless exercises outside your window." Pat, though, was unrepentant. "I'm not ashamed of my body, I'm a naturist and a campaigner for women's lib," she said. The Law didn't agree with her, however, and she was fined £120 for breach of the peace, but even that didn't deter Pat from her running. Just to remind people what all the fuss was about, she started jogging round the block with a T-shirt on, emblazoned with a large "46".

HERE'S THE NUDES

In 1989, Swedish Mikael Sahlin is believed to have become the world's first TV reporter to appear starkers in front of the TV cameras. In only his second assignment on TV, Mikael was reporting on the opening of a new nudist colony near Stockholm and adopted "local costume" to deliver his bulletin. However the report even shocked the liberal Swedes who bombarded the station with protest calls. "I didn't think it was a big deal," said ambitious Mikael. "At first I stood there in my underpants - then I took them off and went ahead with it - anything for the job!"

At last, scientific proof, streaking is contagious.

GIRLS...

BEHAVING...

BADLY.

NUDE DONS

Oxford University student protests took a new twist when a group of girl students raised a stink about college dons showing more than their brainpower in a special garden facing the River Cherwell in the city. Under ancient varsity laws, dons and priests are allowed to strip off in the special area, called Parson's Pleasure. River punters, both students and tourists, got a rude shock when the hot summer of 1990 resulted in the dons showing the world they had more than just large brains. "A number of students have been very upset by the sight," said student chief Henrietta Laing. "It was disgusting to see these old men who we are supposed to respect wobbling around with nothing on," said another student. A woman tour guide who punted past the bathing brainboxes with a group of Japanese tourists said: "I have never known the Japanese to put their cameras away so quickly!"

CHRISTMAS PRESENT

Paul Blacker will never refuse to do the washing up again. When he did after Christmas dinner in 1992, the five furious girl friends he was spending the day with in Cleckheaton, West Yorkshire, decided to give him his just desserts, so they stripped him naked, painted his private parts with green gloss paint and trussed him up like a turkey before tying him to a lamp post!

BARELY A PROTEST

NUDES AGAINST NUKES

In a spontaneous move during a ban the bomb demonstration on Hampstead Heath in 1982, hundreds of people suddenly stripped off their clothes in a "Nudes Against Nukes" gesture to draw attention to their cause. However, it only drew the attention of the police who then had an excuse to move them on, or arrest them.

FULL FRONTAL

Robert Andazola made a full frontal charge when he faced up to police called in to protect renegade workers at a striking Arizona copper mine. The peaceful protest ended up with fires and rock throwing battles. The were 23 workers arrested, including Robert on charges of indecent exposure.

WET BABE

When Ullswater Ski Club was banned from using Ullswater Lake to water ski in 1982, Michelle Howey protested by riding topless in a powerboat across Howtown Bay to the Ullswater Hotel. "I just wanted to show everybody how much the sport has to offer," she said.

DRIVEN TO NUDITY

Around 1,000 worshippers including Prince Michael of Kent and British motor racing ace Stirling Moss were shocked at a Coventry Cathedral service to mark 100 years of the car when a woman stripped naked and shouted: "My mother was killed in a road accident." Angel Koyanti, her nude body daubed all over with anti-car slogans, ran to the front of the cathedral and read an eight-verse poem about the evils of the motor car. She told the congregation: "This is in memory of my mother and others who have died innocent victims. In the spirit of Lady Godiva I am here to mourn the 17 million people killed directly by the car."

ANGRY WOMEN

Even naturists have their militant tendencies. In July 1989 an all-male nude bathing spot in County Dublin was invaded by a large group of women in various states of undress. The exclusive 250-member male swimming club insisted that women were welcome as visitors, but this didn't matter to rock singer Mary Downes who led the protest and had appealed for volunteer protestors on the radio after being allegedly banned from the beach. Chaos ensued as spectators outnumbered demonstrators, causing traffic jams for miles around as 2,000 people jammed the streets leading to the sea.

UNIFORM STRIP

Police beat a bare-bottomed retreat when they failed to stop a procession of nudists in the south Indian town of Bangalore in 1986. Angry members of the public turned on the officers and stripped them naked as they tried to prevent about 200 nude men and women from taking an annual ritual bath. The constables, including two women officers, never recovered their uniforms.

New Labour.
New Traffic Wardens.

Andie McDowell auditioning for 'Groundhog Day'. She got that part too.

BACHELOR OF PARTS

A mystery man ruined the official photo at an Oxford University ball in 1996 when he dropped his trousers as the snap was taken. The cheekie chappie stood, unashamedly, in all his glory, but even with this much showing his identity still mystified dons and undergraduates at Trinity College. One student said: "No one knows who he is and nobody will admit he was their guest."

STREET STREAK

Was he returning those ill-fitting shoes and had forgotten to dress himself, or was he a nude model on his way to a Cambridge student's art class? We'll never know because this mystery man disappeared into the ether and his identity has remained a mystery since he conducted this rather slow-moving streak in 1990. Judging by the reaction of the onlookers he didn't have much to show off anyway.

ATHLETIC TYPES

NUDE KNOCKOUT

In May 1990 more than 100 naturists staged a nude version of It's A Knockout on a farm near Leek, Staffs, in order to raise money for ITV's Telethon charity. They split themselves into teams of six, with at least one women in each, and launched themselves into games like the sack race, water slides and even an egg and spoon race - which, spectators reported, wasn't a pretty sight!

OLYMPIC BREAK IN

At the 1978 Montreal Olympics a streaker sneaked into the stadium and weaved in and out of the dancers during the opening ceremony. "He's not even wearing his accreditation," was all an exasperated Lord Killanin, President of the Olympic International Committee, could bring himself to say.

SPORTING A BLUSH

Sports mistress Claire Page was seen without even a gym slip after pupils at the Queen Elizabeth School in Kirby, Cumbria, discovered a roll of film left in a dark room. The naked truth that Claire was a naturist was exposed by the nosey schoolboys and she was reported to the county's educucation board. Claire was cleared of any misconduct - and now develops all her films at home!

"Darling, it's been ages, how are you?

Phantom of the Whopper.

ON CUE

ON IN A GREEN BLAZE

In March 1990, Christian Hennessy became snooker's first streaker. Wearing just a bow tie and a grin, plus two strategically placed balloons, one emblazoned with "Poll Tax my bum" and other "Hi Mum, happy Mother's Day", he strut his stuff in front of millions of TV viewers at the Canada-Northern Ireland match in Bournemouth in March 1990. Bingo caller Christian then kissed referee Len Ganley on the nose before police arrived and he was arrested for indecent exposure.

TRIPLE WHAMMY

The sight of three attractive women running down the road at full pelt is enough to turn anyone's head, especially when they are totally starkers. It turned out the three were bride-to-be Karen Laight and her bridesmaids Mandy Sayce and Karen's sister Lorraine having fun after a riotous hen party in Tamworth, Staffs in March 1983. A police patrol turned a blind eye after they caught up with them as they streaked through the streets, but the local cab drivers were less charitable. They broadcast news of the sighting over the radio and cabs by the dozen turned up to offer their services. Not surprisingly, the girls refused and opted to jog the last mile home - followed by a number of cabbies, just in case the girls changed their minds, of course.

ANYTHING ELSE MADAM?

Retired businessman Ged Speight served up more than just cocktails when he handed out drinks at a bash for landladies - because he was only wearing a bow tie. Seventeen stone Ged and his mates were unhappy about being put into a small side bar while the landlady entertained a group from the Licensed Victuallers Association, so he stripped off, grabbed a tray of drinks and burst in on the gathering to celebrate the opening of a new restaurant-bar at the Bexley Arms in Windsor, Berks in July 1995. "They all looked like Bet out of Coronation Street," said Ged. "They were putting on airs and graces as if they were Royalty, when suddenly my beer gut appeared at the end of the table. I asked 'will there be anything else', wiggled my bum and walked back into the bar to cheers from the lads. The only complaint was from one landlady who couldn't get her glasses on in time." Landlady Anne Chesney said: "I threatened to bar him but he said he would start a naked picket so I let him off with a warning."

"Hands up all those who think I'm attractive".

PLENTY DOWN UNDER

Even before the 1990 Commonwealth Games had started, there were some memorable performances from the Australian team. Two unnamed Antipodeans showed plenty of Down Under when they excelled in the naked 50-metre dash, creating screams of shock from female athletes wandering through the normally tranquil Olympic Village. The two were never caught as no-one could remember their faces!

100-METRE FLASH

British naturists are planning to ready, steady and get 'em off in the first nude Olympics in the year 2,000. "We want the Olympics to coincide with a hundred years of naturism in the year 2,000," said British naturism magazine editor Rex Watson. "There are sports like boules and mini tennis that naturists specialise in, but otherwise we'll do all the sports you'd find in the normal Olympics - the competitors will just have to be extra careful during baton changes. And, obviously, we'd need to hold the event in a warm climate," he added, with an eye on his lunchbox.

JUST REWARDS

CHILLY PRIZE

Workmates cheered on Stuart Dancer as he threw off his clothes, stepped on to a pair of skis and whizzed across the snow to win £1,000 worth of new carpets in the winter of 1985. The factory worker made his naked dash across an industrial estate to the carpet warehouse at Brackley, Northants, which had offered the prize to anyone who skied there in the nude.

HOW MUCH

In 1990 Playgirl magazine declared that it was ready to offer Prince Charles £300,000 to pose nude for its centrefold. Playgirl bosses said they were eventually willing to offer the sum to ten men they would most like to see starkers. They rest were international sex symbols Sean Connery, Tom Cruise, Mel Gibson, MIkhail Gorbachev (why?), Eddie Murphy, Paul Newman, Jack Nicholson, Bruce Springsteen and Michael Jordan. Other stars who have reportedly turned down offers from Playgirl include George Hamilton, who was offered £25,000 for an afternoon's work, Tom Jones, Englebert Humperdink and Burt Reynolds.

UNIDENTIFIED MODEL

An unofficial guidebook to the Hampshire towns of Gosport and Fareham, featuring a nude model posing at several tourist attractions in the area, was first branded "disgusting" by the towns' two Mayors and then banned in the early 1980s after a legal wrangle over copywright. Yet Fareham's Mayor, Roger Price, failed to recognise the shapely model just a couple of months after the incident and picked her as beauty queen for the same town! The model concerned, Michelle Shepherd, said it was ironic, because she even sat on the Mayor's knee when she was declared the winner!

SCARED TO BE BEAR

The sight of a man walking around with no trousers scared the pants off two huge bears at London Zoo in 1983. The man got into their enclosure by climbing a wall and when he took off his clothes the two bears, weighing ten hundred weight between them, couldn't stand the grizzly sight and ran, cowering, to their keeper until the panic was over. The man was rescued safely and later released by police.

THEY'RE OFF!

Stephen Brighton's streak at the 1995 News Handicap Hurdle at Fontwell nearly ended in tragedy when he was struck by one of the horses. Richard Dunwoody, who was leading the field, clouted Brighton with his whip to try and get him off the course, but the galloping nude was then struck by Rodney Farrant's horse, Boxing Match. The 29-year-old barman was unhurt, but Dunwoody was angry, saying: "He was stupid - he could have been hurt and so could we."

TOURIST ATTRACTIONS

BEAUTS ONLY

Tropea, an Italian fishing village on the southern coast of Calabria, brought ridicule on itself in 1982 when, in an attempt to become a rival to St Tropez, the town councillors voted to prohibit nudity on the beaches, "excepting the nudity of a beautiful woman, young if possible, and capable of exalting the beauty and the femininity of her body". The uproar it caused was such that the Mayor, Guiseppe Romano was obliged to explain at a press conference that the new rule was needed "to prevent abberrant situations which could annoy or disgust some people."

FACING A STERN LECTURE

Oxford Student Jocelyn Witchard was nearly sent down when she plunged off the town's Magdelen Bridge starkers in 1995. And her tutors at the all-woman college of St Hilda's were even less amused when they saw pictures of Jocelyn in tabloid newspapers the next day. "There hasn't been a problem with male students taking their kit off and jumping off the bridge," said Jocelyn. "I think what I did was good for the college. It does have a reputation for being a bit stuffy and jolly hockey sticks."

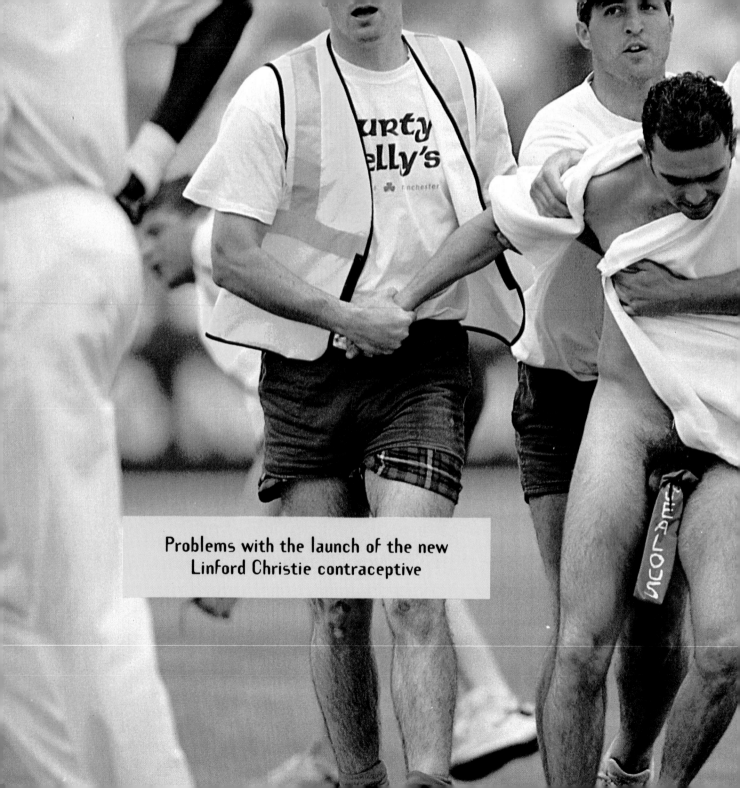

Problems with the launch of the new
Linford Christie contraceptive

NAKED CONFESSIONS

BARING ALL

It's not hard for the Reverend Ronald Atkins to get people to bare more than their soul - for he is a nudist. He told Health and Efficiency magazine that people find it easier to confess without clothes on, quoting one person who confessed to killing his own wife because, it turned out, she had commited suicide because of his extra-marital affair. "He wouldn't have confessed if we hadn't been in the state of pure relaxation that nudism brings," said the Reverend.

INDECENT ACT

A rector shocked his church members and other local residents in 1982 when he suggested in a parish newsletter that everyone should strip naked at beaches, public swimming baths or even on country walks. Canon William Metcalfe of Bottlesford, Notts, was pronouncing his theory for ridding the world of sleazy strip clubs, rapists, prostitutes and pornography. "They are generally suffering only from an imposed form of frustration," he said. "All we need is an Act of Parliament saying that stripping off in public is not indecent exposure." His parish didn't agree though and one spokesman, a local farmer, said: "I don't want the rector or any of the local villagers running naked over my fields. There has to be a limit and I draw the line at public nudity."

STORM IN A D-CUP

The Royal Navy scotched any suggestions that the crew of one of its submarines had acted improperly when it anchored off a nudist beach in the summer of 1982 and promptly upped periscope for a free peep show. "HMS Porpoise came inshore to escape heavy shipping in thick fog," said an indignant Royal Navy spokesman - despite the fact that Britain was enjoying clear weather and a mini-heatwave at the time.

BIT OF ALL WIGHT

A group of women on the Isle of Wight caused a storm of controversy in 1995 when they starred in a saucy seaside calender that obscured their faces. The £7.95 calenders, limited to 1,000 editions, were sold out in no time as husbands and boyfriends snapped them up to see if they could recognise their loved ones revealing all for cameraman Dave Betts. "It was all done in the best possible taste," said Dave. "I'm surprised it has caused such an uproar."

GOOD NUDE GUIDE

Naturists in America have taken a fig-leaf out of Egon Ronay's book and produced their own Good Nudes Guide. The book lists more than 1,000 places around the world where naturists are welcomed. Some of the more way-out spots recommended include Alaska, where nudism is booming and The Polar Bear Society in the Arctic Ocean, which offers free membership to anyone who dares to swim nude in the freezing sea, although, while you might get membership, you might also lose a member

CLEANING UP

Former store detective Richard Stead had enough of being on the dole after five months out of work, so he advertised his services as a naked house cleaner. The 6ft 4in bachelor charged £15 a time and peeled off as many clothes as his clients wanted before buffing their ornaments, hoovering their shagpiles and washing the crockery as quick as a flash. "I suppose a lot of women book me for the novelty value," he said. "But I always warn them, there is no hanky panky. I've had a great response. Husbands book me as a birthday surprise for their wives and other women hire me for a laugh and invite their pals to watch. I don't get at all embarrassed - as a naturist I spend all my spare time in the buff."

PULL THE OTHER ONE

Part-time Aussie model, Jade, gave the regulars at The Victoria pub in Batley, West Yorkshire, a rare treat in 1995, pulling pints topless for half an hour before discovering she was in the wrong pub! When the 6ft student turned up at The Victoria and asked where to get changed, landlord Mick Nolan immediately twigged that Jade should have been a mile down the road at another Victoria pub which was having a "topless night", but had been sent by an agency and dropped at the wrong pub by a cabby. He ushered her in and told her the way to go. "I thought it would be a nice treat for the lads," said the cheeky proprietor. "When she began serving topless the lads thought it was great - she was really beautiful with a great body. When I told her the truth she wouldn't believe me, then she called me a mongrel. Now I'm considering hiring topless barmaids too."

ROD AND TACKLE

Dozens of naturist fishermen did their best to avoid flying hooks when they took part in Britain's first nude anglers event at Garden Farm Fishery near Barlestone, Leicestershire in July 1994. Thistles, nettles and insects also meant that the fishermen had to tread very carefully or risk some nasty stings down below. Screens were also put up to avoid local villagers walking the towpath netting a nasty shock!

THE BIG STRIPPER

When the world's tallest rollercoaster, The Big One, opened in Blackpool in 1994, but no one could have foreseen the new craze it would start - girls flashing their boobs on it for the overhead cameras! Perhaps it should have been renamed The Big Two, because the bare-devil riders, as they have become known, just love stripping off at 85mph just for the thrill of feeling their chests wobble at 3g! One rollercoaster worker said: "There can't be another white-knuckle ride like it - we're now calling it the white nipple ride!"

OUTFOXED

Posh huntsmen from the Vine and Craven Hunt at Lambourne, Berks, found themselves on a goose chase in 1984 when they agreed to act as extras in a shoot for, supposedly, a French fashion magazine.

It all seemed perfectly above board as an ice-cool model turned up in riding breeches, hat and hunting jacket, sipping from the traditional stirrup cup and casually chatted to the huntsmen before the "off". But then the model whipped off her outfit, leapt naked on to her horse and galloped off across the fields. Staff of the magazine Men Only had outfoxed the hunt members with their fashion shoot ruse and the galloping nude along with a naked romp in a stable, appeared in the next edition. "After the initial shock I think we all quite enjoyed it," said one hunt member, "although I don't know what our wives will think of it all."

DEMONSTRATION STRIP

Amanda Green decided to come out in sympathy with Arthur Scargill's striking miners in 1984...so she took her top off! The 15,000 demonstrating pitmen couldn't believe their eyes when Amanda pulled down her T-shirt and paraded up and down with a patrolling police sergeant. Busty Amanda, daughter of a mine maintenance worker, said: "People were jeering and shouting at the miners so I decided to cheer them up."

What a big-hearted girl!

Eurovision Dong Contest 2
1st entry - Still Nil Points

IF YOU ENJOYED THIS BOOK, WHAT ABOUT THESE!

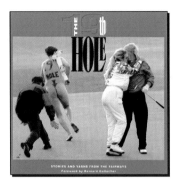

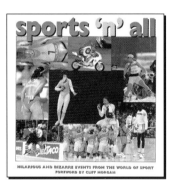

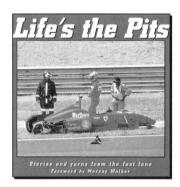

All these books are available at your local book shop or can be ordered direct from the publisher. Just list the titles you require and give your name address, including post code. Prices and availability are subject to change without notice.

Please send to Chameleon Cash Sales, 106 Great Russell Street London WCIB 3LJ, a cheque or postal order for £7.99 and add the following for postage and packaging:

UK - £1.00 For the first book. 50p for the second and 30p for the third for each additional book up to a maximum of £3.00.
OVERSEAS -(including Eire) £2.00 For the first book and £1.00 for the second and 50p for each additional book up to a maximum of £3.00.